My Problem Isn't Your Problem

By

Larry Richman

CENTURY PUBLISHING

SALT LAKE CITY, UTAH

My Problem Isn't Your Problem

ISBN 978-0-941846-36-3

Portions of this book were developed with the assistance of generative artificial intelligence tools to support idea generation, editing, and organization. All content has been reviewed, curated, and refined by the author to ensure originality, clarity, and quality.

centurypubl.com

info@centurypubl.com

Printed in the United States of America.

Contents

Preface

We all have problems. But not everyone takes responsibility for them. It's easier to blame. Blame the economy, your boss, your spouse, or the system.

But here's the truth: if it's your problem, it's your job to fix it.

That doesn't mean everything is your fault. But it is your responsibility to respond—to take ownership of your part, your actions, your mindset, and your next step.

This book is about the quiet power of personal responsibility. It's about owning your mess instead of blaming others. It's about facing the hard truth that no one is coming to rescue you—and realizing that's actually good news. Because once you stop waiting for someone else to change, you can start changing what matters: you.

Why We Avoid Responsibility

Taking ownership feels risky. It exposes us. If we admit we're part of the problem, we also admit we have work to do—and that's uncomfortable.

So, we protect ourselves with excuses:

- "It's not my job."
- "They should have told me."
- "It's just how I was raised."
- "If they would just listen, this wouldn't be happening."

Excuses may make us feel safe. But they also keep us stuck. This book will help you break out of that cycle.

What You'll Learn

In the chapters ahead, you'll explore what it means to take full ownership of your challenges—and how doing so changes everything. You'll learn to:

- Spot the subtle ways you avoid responsibility.
- Challenge blame, excuses, and entitlement.
- Focus on what you can control.
- Separate your identity from your outcomes.
- Stop worrying about what others think.
- Lead yourself with honesty and courage

You'll find practical tools, reflection prompts, and real-world stories from people who made progress—not by waiting for others to change, but by choosing to lead themselves first.

The Payoff of Ownership

When you take ownership of your problems, you regain power. You stop spinning in frustration. You stop wasting energy trying to fix others. You stop waiting for perfect conditions.

Instead, you start solving what's yours to solve. And that's where growth begins.

If you've ever felt stuck, overlooked, frustrated, or burned out…

If you've ever wanted change but felt helpless to make it happen…

This book is for you.

Because your life won't change until you do.

And that starts here—with ownership.

CHAPTER 1

The Blame Game

Why we point fingers—and what it costs us.

We've all done it. Your project falls apart, and you blame your team. You miss a deadline, and you blame your calendar. You snap at someone, and you blame your stress—or their attitude.

Blame is easy. It feels safe. It takes the pressure off. But blame also takes away your power. Because the moment you make your problem someone else's fault, you give away your ability to fix it.

Blame Is a Distraction

Imagine this: A restaurant's online reviews are terrible. The owner blames the customers—"They're too picky." She blames her staff—"They're not working hard enough." She even blames the food delivery apps—"They're the reason we're slow."

But she never asks the kitchen how long dishes take. She never checks how orders are packed. She never asks customers for feedback.

And nothing changes. Why? Because she's solving the wrong problem—everyone else's.

The Real Problem with Blame

Blame feels productive. It feels like we're doing something—
analyzing, reacting, responding. But really, we're avoiding.
Avoiding responsibility. Avoiding discomfort. Avoiding the
truth. Blame turns attention away from the one thing you can
control: you.

And while you're pointing fingers, your problem sits there,
growing roots.

What Blame Sounds Like

Blame shows up in subtle ways. You might hear yourself
saying:
- "If they would just…"
- "It's not fair because…"
- "They always…"
- "I wouldn't have to if they hadn't…"
- "There's nothing I can do because…"

Each of these statements has one thing in common: They put
the solution out there—with someone else.

And as long as the solution lives with someone else, your
problem won't go away.

A Story: The Sales Slump

Jason worked in sales. His numbers dropped for three straight
months. He blamed the economy. He blamed the leads. He
blamed his boss for raising the target.

Eventually, his manager asked a simple question: "What part
of this do you own?"

Jason bristled. Then paused. He realized he hadn't followed up with his warm leads. He'd been avoiding hard conversations. And he'd stopped preparing before calls.

The economy might be slow. But his effort was slower.

That shift—from blame to ownership—helped Jason turn his slump around. He didn't wait for the market to get better. He got better.

Blame Feels Good—Until It Doesn't

Blame helps us avoid guilt or embarrassment. It lets us protect our ego. But the cost is steep.

Blame blocks learning. Blame poisons relationships. Blame keeps us stuck. When you live in blame, every problem becomes someone else's job to fix.

But when you own your part—even if it's just 10%—you open the door to change.

What Ownership Looks Like

Taking ownership doesn't mean you take the blame for everything. It means asking:

- What did I contribute to this situation?
- What choices did I make?
- What could I do differently next time?

Ownership shifts the focus from who's at fault to what can I learn? And that shift changes everything.

> **Key Takeaway**
> Blame feels easier than ownership, but it costs you your power. When you stop pointing fingers and start asking better questions, you take the first step toward real change.

Reflection

Take a few minutes to write about one problem you are currently facing. Then ask: Who or what am I blaming?

_____

_____

_____

_____

_____

What part of this might be mine to own?

_____

_____

_____

_____

If I stopped blaming, what action could I take today?

_____

_____

_____

_____

CHAPTER 2

Excuses Are Easy

Why we make them, how they hold us back,
and what to do instead.

We all make excuses.

- "I didn't have time."
- "That's just how I am."
- "No one told me."
- "I'm not good with technology."
- "It's not my fault."

Excuses sound like reasons. But most of the time, they're not. They're shields. They protect us from the discomfort of failure, the fear of judgment, and the hard work of change. But they also protect us from progress.

A Story: The Missed Promotion

Tina wanted a promotion. She had the experience, the tenure, and the desire. But when someone else got the job, she was furious.

"They always promote the favorites," she said. "It's because I don't play politics." "I didn't even know they were considering candidates."

At first, Tina vented to her friends. Then she started blaming her manager. But finally, a colleague pulled her aside and asked: "Did you ever tell your boss you were interested in the role?"

Tina paused. She hadn't.

She assumed her work would speak for itself. Excuses had protected her pride—but they also hid the fact that she hadn't taken initiative. When she finally had an honest conversation with her manager, her manager said, "I didn't know you wanted it. I would've considered you if you'd said something."

Next time, she did. And she got the job.

Why We Make Excuses

Excuses are easier than effort. They're more comfortable than change. And they make us feel safe—at least in the short term.

But underneath most excuses is something deeper:

- Fear of failure
- Fear of rejection
- Fear of not being enough

So, we tell ourselves stories to avoid the sting:

- "It wasn't fair."
- "It wouldn't have worked anyway."
- "It's not worth the effort."

These stories protect our ego. But they also trap our potential.

Excuses vs. Explanations

Let's be clear: not every reason is an excuse. Life happens. There are real barriers and not everything is under your control.

The difference is how you respond.

- **An explanation** describes reality so you can adjust.
- **An excuse** uses reality to avoid responsibility.

Explanation: "I missed the deadline because I underestimated the time. Next time, I'll start earlier."

Excuse: "I missed the deadline because everything takes too long, and people kept bothering me. It's not my fault."

One owns the problem. The other dodges it.

What Excuses Sound Like

Excuses often show up in subtle ways. They might sound like:

- "I just don't have the time."
- "That's not my skill set."
- "They should've told me."
- "I tried that once and it didn't work."
- "That's just the way things are."

Each of these statements may contain a sliver of truth. But if it stops you from acting, it's still an excuse.

Excuses in Disguise

Some excuses wear professional clothes. They sound like smart strategy:

- "Let's wait until the timing is perfect."
- "I'll do it when things calm down."
- "We need more data before we move forward."

But deep down, they're often just fear with a fresh coat of paint. Progress rarely waits for perfect conditions.

The Cost of Excuses

Excuses feel good in the moment. They relieve pressure. They explain away discomfort. But they also:

- Delay growth
- Erode trust

- Lower your standards
- Limit your opportunities

Over time, excuses shrink your life.

- You stop reaching.
- You stop risking.
- You settle.

And worst of all, you start to believe your own story—that you're not capable, not ready, not worth it.

A Better Way: Radical Honesty

If you want to grow, you need to replace excuses with honest reflection. Try this:

1. **Notice the excuse.** Ask: "What story am I telling myself right now?"
2. **Name the fear.** Ask: "What am I afraid of? Failing? Looking bad? Feeling stupid?"
3. **Own your choice.** Say: "I chose not to prepare." Or: "I let fear win." Or: "I didn't prioritize this."

It's hard. It's humbling. But it's also freeing. Because once you name it, you can change it.

Key Takeaway

Excuses protect you from discomfort—but they also protect you from growth. When you stop explaining away your problems and start owning them, you gain the power to change.

Reflection

What excuses do I tend to use when things go wrong?

_____

_____

_____

_____

_____

What fear or discomfort might be hiding underneath those excuses?

_____

_____

_____

_____

_____

What would change if I replaced those excuses with action or ownership?

_____

_____

_____

_____

_____

CHAPTER 3

The Ownership Shift

What it looks like to move from blame to responsibility.

You can't solve a problem you won't own. You can analyze it. Complain about it. Blame others for it. Even build your whole identity around it.

But until you take ownership, nothing changes.

Ownership is the shift from saying, "This isn't fair,"
to asking, "What can I do now?"

It's not always easy. But it's always empowering.

A Story: The Team Conflict

Nina led a small team in a growing company. Tension was high. Deadlines were missed. People were snapping at each other. She blamed the team's attitude. She tried team-building exercises. She added pep talks. She asked HR for advice. Nothing worked.

Then someone asked her a hard question: "Have you taken a look at how you're leading?"

At first, she resisted. She was working hard. She cared about the team. But when she looked closer, she realized something: She hadn't been clear about expectations. She rarely followed up. She avoided hard conversations. She had been managing tasks—not leading people.

Once she took ownership, she started making small changes: Clearer goals. One-on-ones. Honest feedback. And the team started to shift too. Not because they changed first—because she did.

The Path to Ownership

Taking ownership doesn't mean blaming yourself for everything. It means recognizing your part. Even if someone else started the fire, what did you add to the flames? Even if the situation is unfair, how are you responding to it?

Here's what ownership sounds like:
- "I didn't communicate that clearly."
- "I chose not to follow up."
- "I avoided that conversation."
- "I wasn't as prepared as I thought."

It's simple. It's honest. And it's powerful.

Why Ownership Is Hard

Ownership is hard because it asks us to do three things we naturally resist:

1. **Be honest with ourselves.** That means naming our own mistakes and blind spots.
2. **Face discomfort.** Taking ownership often leads us to things we'd rather avoid—apologizing, changing habits, doing hard work.
3. **Give up excuses.** We lose the comforting lie that "it's all someone else's fault."

But in exchange, we get something better: progress.

The Responsibility Ladder

Here's a tool you can use. It's called the Responsibility Ladder—a simple way to see where you are when facing a challenge:

Step	Mindset
Blame	"It's their fault."
Excuse	"There was nothing I could do."
Wait	"Maybe it will get better on its own."
Acknowledge	"This isn't working."
Accept	"I see my part in this."
Act	"Here's what I can do next."
Own	"I am responsible for my results."

The goal is to move up the ladder—to shift from reacting to leading.

Where are you right now? And what would help you take the next step?

A Shift in Thinking

When you take ownership, you stop asking:
- "Who is to blame?"
- "Why is this happening to me?"
- "Why won't they change?"

And you start asking:
- "What's mine to fix?"
- "What can I learn here?"
- "What's the next right step I can take?"

That shift moves you from stuck to strong. From passive to powerful.

Ownership and Identity

Sometimes we resist ownership because we think it says something bad about who we are.

- "If I admit I messed up, I'm a failure."
- "If I own the problem, people will think I'm weak."
- "If I take responsibility, I'm letting others off the hook."

But ownership doesn't make you weak. It makes you trustworthy.

People respect those who take responsibility. It shows character. It builds credibility. It invites others to do the same.

And it's the only real path to growth.

Key Takeaway

Ownership isn't about taking the blame. It's about taking control. When you stop waiting for others to change and start owning your role, you take back the power to shape your outcomes.

Reflection

What is a problem I've been avoiding responsibility for?

_____

_____

_____

_____

_____

What part of this situation do I actually control?

_____

_____

_____

_____

_____

What action could I take today that reflects ownership?

_____

_____

_____

_____

_____

CHAPTER 4

What Is in My Control?

How to stop spinning your wheels and start where you actually have power.

Life throws a lot at us: Deadlines. Disagreements. Delays. A tough boss. A sick child. A sudden change. Expectations you didn't agree to. Pressures you didn't ask for.

It's easy to feel stuck or overwhelmed—especially when so much seems out of your hands.

But here's the key to progress: Focus on what is in your control.

Let go of what's not.

That's where power lives.

A Story: The Job Search Spiral

Andre lost his job when his company downsized. He applied for dozens of positions but heard nothing back. He grew frustrated. Then resentful. Then hopeless. He started saying things like:

- "No one is hiring."
- "It's all about who you know."
- "I'm too old for this market."
- "I guess I'm just out of luck."

Then a friend asked him a hard question: "What's one thing you can do today to move forward?"

He paused. Then replied, "I can revise my resume. I can practice my interviews. I can reach out to three people."

The next day, he did just that.

The job offers didn't come instantly—but something shifted. Andre went from helpless to focused. From stuck to steady. Because he took action where he could—and let go of where he couldn't.

The Circle of Control

Try this simple tool. Picture three circles:

1. **Circle of Control.** Things you can directly influence. *Your actions, choices, words, time, attitude, effort.*
2. **Circle of Influence.** Things you can affect but not control. *Other people's behavior, decisions, team dynamics, company culture.*
3. **Circle of Concern.** Things you care about but can't change. *The weather. The past. Global events. Other people's opinions.*

The more energy you spend inside the Circle of Control, the more progress you make.

The more energy you spend outside it, the more frustrated you become.

Why We Focus on the Wrong Circle

Focusing on what we can't control gives us something to complain about—but nothing to change. It feels active—but it's just noise.

Why do we do it?

- It distracts us from our own responsibility.
- It gives us someone to blame.
- It keeps us from risking failure.

- It lets us stay stuck—but comfortable.

But growth starts where excuses end: inside the circle you control.

What's Really in Your Control

You can't control your boss. But you *can* control how prepared you are for meetings.

You can't control the economy. But you *can* control your spending and upskilling.

You can't control your spouse's mood. But you *can* control your reactions, boundaries, and tone.

You can't control the past. But you *can* control how you learn from it.

Every day, you choose how you show up—even when circumstances are hard.

The Power of Shifting Your Focus

Let's look at how shifting from what you *can't* control to what you *can* actually works.

Focus On This	Instead of This
Your schedule	Other people's priorities
Your response	Their bad attitude
Your effort	The outcome you wish you had
Your preparation	Last-minute emergencies
Your boundaries	How others treat you
Your words	What people assume

Every shift above creates forward motion.

A Simple Practice: The Control Sort

When you're overwhelmed, pause and write down:

- Everything that's bothering you.
- Next to each item, mark: C (Control), I (Influence), or O (Outside).

Now cross out everything marked O.

Underline everything marked C.

Take one action today from the "C" list.

This tiny exercise grounds you in reality and activates momentum.

A Story: The Morning Chaos

Sandra's mornings were always chaotic. The kids weren't ready. The house was a mess. She was late for work. Every day started with stress and yelling.

She kept saying, "My kids never listen," and "We're just not morning people."

But one day, she took a step back and asked: "What can I control?"

She realized she could:

- Prepare backpacks the night before.
- Wake up 20 minutes earlier.
- Create a simple morning checklist for the kids.

It didn't fix everything overnight—but things got better. Because she stopped fighting her family's behavior—and started owning her response.

Key Takeaway

You can't control everything. But you can control something. And when you focus your energy there, you start to move forward—no matter what's happening around you.

Reflection

What am I trying to control that I actually can't?

_____

_____

_____

_____

_____

What's one small action I *can* take today?

_____

_____

_____

_____

What would change if I focused only on what I control?

_____

_____

_____

_____

_____

CHAPTER 5

Internal vs. External Validation

Why your worth doesn't depend on what others think.

You did the hard thing. You spoke up in the meeting. You launched the new idea. You set a boundary. You took ownership.

And then… silence. Or worse, criticism. Suddenly, you're second-guessing:

- "Did I do the right thing?"
- "What will they think of me?"
- "Should I just go back to playing it safe?"

This is the trap of external validation.

When your confidence depends on other people's approval, you'll never feel steady—because their opinion will always shift.

But when your validation comes from within, you stop chasing applause and start building confidence that lasts.

The Problem with Chasing Approval

We all want to be liked. That's human. We want our ideas to be heard, our efforts to be seen, and our presence to be appreciated.

But if we need approval to feel okay, we become controlled by it.

- We over-explain.
- We hold back.
- We shrink our voice to fit someone else's comfort zone.

And when they don't notice—or don't agree—we feel crushed.

That's not confidence. That's performance.

A Story: The Presentation That Flopped

Jordan spent weeks preparing a company-wide presentation. He put his best ideas forward and felt great about it—until someone in the back row yawned halfway through. Suddenly, Jordan spiraled.

- "Was I boring?"
- "Did I say something wrong?"
- "Did I mess this up?"

Afterward, he asked a few trusted colleagues for honest feedback. They told him it was one of the clearest, most helpful talks they'd heard.

The problem wasn't his performance. The problem was where he placed his focus: on the one disinterested person instead of the value he brought.

External reactions are unpredictable. Internal clarity is steady.

What External Validation Looks Like

You may be relying on external validation if you find yourself:

- Constantly asking, "Was that okay?"
- Changing your opinion to match the room.
- Needing praise to feel competent.
- Avoiding conflict to avoid judgment.

- Doubting your worth without affirmation.

The danger? You start shaping your decisions around what others might think—not what you believe is right.

What Internal Validation Looks Like

Internal validation comes from alignment with your values and integrity. It sounds like:

- "I did what I believe is right."
- "I'm proud of how I handled that."
- "I learned something, even if others didn't notice."
- "I can improve, but I still respect myself."

You may still want feedback—but you're no longer dependent on it.

How to Build Internal Validation

1. Know Your Values

When your actions align with your values, you gain peace—even if others disagree. Ask:

- What matters most to me?
- What kind of person do I want to be in this situation?

2. Reflect Before You React

Instead of asking, "Did they like it?" try:

- Was I honest?
- Was I thoughtful?
- Did I give my best?

Let that be your measure of success.

3. Catch the Comparison

Every time you think, "They're better than me," reframe it: "I can learn from them without devaluing myself."

4. Celebrate Quiet Wins

You don't need applause to acknowledge growth.

- You followed through? That counts.
- You kept a promise to yourself? That matters.

Start seeing yourself—not others—as the one who gets to decide whether you're enough.

A Story: The Entrepreneur's Choice

Layla launched a side business designing custom planners. Her friends loved the idea—but when she posted it online, it didn't get many likes. She almost shut it down.

But instead, she asked herself: "Do I still believe in this?" The answer was yes.

So, she kept going. She improved her marketing. She listened to real customers. And her business grew—not because everyone approved, but because *she* did.

Key Takeaway

External validation is unreliable fuel. Internal validation is your steady engine. When you stop chasing applause and start trusting your own integrity, you'll lead with courage—not fear.

Reflection

What am I doing right now mainly to gain approval?

_____

_____

_____

_____

_____

How do I react when others don't praise or agree with me?

_____

_____

_____

_____

_____

What would it look like to validate myself—before anyone else does?

_____

_____

_____

_____

_____

CHAPTER 6

Identity and Responsibility

Why what you believe about yourself shapes what you take responsibility for.

We all have a story about who we are. Some of it is inherited. Some of it is learned. And much of it runs quietly in the background—shaping how we think, what we say yes to, and what we avoid.

Your identity is the story you tell yourself about yourself.

And here's the catch: That story affects how you handle problems.

The Hidden Link Between Identity and Ownership

If you believe you're always the helper, you'll struggle to say no. If you believe you're not good with money, you'll avoid financial decisions. If you believe you're a failure, you'll hesitate to try again. If you believe "this is just how I am," you'll stop trying to grow.

What we *believe* about ourselves becomes what we *expect* of ourselves.

And those expectations set the limits for what we're willing to take responsibility for.

A Story: The Overloaded Volunteer

Maria volunteered for everything—at work, in her community, at church. She said yes to every request, even when she was tired or overwhelmed.

Her identity? "I'm the one who shows up." It made her dependable—but also exhausted and resentful.

When her mentor asked, "What would happen if you said no?" she froze. "They'd think I'm selfish. I wouldn't be who I'm supposed to be."

Her story was clear: good people sacrifice. Rest means weakness. Saying no means you're letting others down.

But none of that was actually true.

Once she started rewriting the story—"I can care for others *and* care for myself"—she learned to set boundaries without guilt.

Her identity shifted. And so did her behavior.

The Stories We Live By

We all carry stories like:

- "I'm just not a leader."
- "I always mess things up."
- "I'm not creative."
- "I'm the one who has to fix things."
- "I'm not the kind of person who asks for help."

These beliefs might sound like facts, but they're really habits of thought.

And until you question them, they'll quietly shape how much responsibility you take—or avoid.

Rewriting the Story

Changing your behavior starts with changing your beliefs.

Here's how to do that:

1. Name the Story

Ask: What am I telling myself about who I am in this situation?

Examples:

- "I'm too emotional to be in charge."
- "I always get walked on."
- "I don't do confrontation."

2. Challenge the Story

Ask:

- Is this actually true?
- Where did I learn this?
- What would happen if I believed something different?

3. Choose a Better Identity

Instead of: "I'm bad with money," try: "I'm learning to manage money well."

Instead of: "I'm a people pleaser," try: "I'm someone who values honesty and healthy boundaries."

You're not lying to yourself. You're giving yourself permission to grow.

A Story: The Silent Manager

David was a new team leader who struggled to speak up. He avoided giving feedback and rarely shared opinions in meetings.

His story? "I'm not a strong communicator. I'm more of a behind-the-scenes guy."

But his silence was holding the team back. When his coach asked him to reflect on that belief, David realized it came from childhood—being told to stay quiet, not cause trouble, not stand out. He wasn't "bad at communicating." He was just uncomfortable being visible.

Over time, he practiced short updates in meetings. He gave one piece of feedback per week.

He didn't become a loud leader—but he became a clear one.

And it started by shifting his identity.

Responsibility Follows Identity

When you see yourself as capable, you start acting like it.

When you believe you're powerless, you wait for others to fix things.

When you own your identity, you own your impact.

Responsibility doesn't just come from willpower. It comes from knowing who you are—and choosing who you want to become.

Key Takeaway
You act in line with what you believe about yourself. If you want to take more responsibility, rewrite the story—because ownership begins with identity.

Reflection

What roles or labels am I carrying that shape how I act?

_____

_____

_____

_____

What story do I tell myself when I avoid taking responsibility?

_____

_____

_____

_____

What identity would support the kind of action I want to take?

_____

_____

_____

_____

CHAPTER 7

Owning It at Work, Home, and Life

What personal responsibility looks like in the real world.

It's easy to talk about ownership in theory. It's harder to practice when you're tired, stressed, or frustrated—and still expected to show up.

But this is where it matters most: not in big speeches or dramatic breakthroughs, but in the everyday moments when you choose to lead yourself instead of blaming others.

Let's look at how ownership plays out in three common areas: work, home, and life.

At Work: From Frustration to Initiative

Scenario: The Unclear Project

You're working on a project, but no one gave clear expectations. You feel stuck—and annoyed. It's tempting to say: "They didn't tell me what to do. Not my fault if it goes wrong."

But ownership sounds like: "I need clarity. I'll ask for it instead of waiting."

You schedule a 10-minute check-in with your manager. You summarize what you think is expected and ask for feedback. Suddenly, you're back on track.

Ownership isn't about having all the answers. It's about taking the first step to find them.

Scenario: The Tough Coworker

You work with someone who constantly criticizes your ideas in meetings. You feel disrespected and resentful. The blame script says: "They're the problem. They need to change."

Ownership asks: "How can I respond in a way I'm proud of?"

Maybe you clarify your ideas more clearly before meetings. Maybe you ask for feedback privately. Maybe you set boundaries or involve a mediator.

You don't control their behavior. But you do control your response.

At Home: From Guilt to Responsibility

Scenario: The Tense Relationship

You and your spouse keep having the same argument. You say, "She never listens." She says, "You always overreact."

You think the problem is her. She thinks the problem is you.

But ownership steps in and asks: "What part of this cycle do I contribute to?"

Maybe you interrupt too quickly. Maybe you assume the worst. Maybe you avoid hard conversations.

You don't need to take all the blame to take some of the responsibility.

And that shift often opens the door for real dialogue.

Scenario: The Parenting Struggle

Your teenager is always on her phone. Chores aren't done. Schoolwork is missing. You're frustrated—and exhausted. You say, "She's lazy."

But pause. Ask: "Have I been clear? Consistent? Calm?" Maybe the rules change too often. Maybe she is confused by mixed signals. Maybe she is testing limits—as teens do—and what she needs is your steadiness, not your stress.

Ownership in parenting doesn't mean control. It means modeling what responsibility looks like.

In Life: From Helpless to Empowered

Scenario: The Health Wake-Up Call

Your doctor gives you hard news. You need to lose weight, reduce stress, or manage your blood pressure. It's tempting to say: "I don't have time." "I don't like exercise." "Healthy food is expensive."

All true—but none of it solves the problem.

Ownership says: "I can walk 15 minutes a day." "I can learn one new recipe each week." "I can manage what I do control."

You don't need to overhaul your life overnight. You just need to take one step today.

Scenario: The Stuck Season

You feel like nothing is working. You're uninspired. Directionless. Lost.

Blame says: "Life is unfair. Other people have it easier."

Ownership says: "I don't need all the answers to take one small action."

Maybe it's journaling. Calling a friend. Updating your resume. Taking a break from social media.

You don't need to control the future. You just need to own your next move.

Ownership Is a Practice

Personal responsibility isn't about being perfect. It's about showing up, again and again, with honesty and intention.

Sometimes that means apologizing. Sometimes it means drawing a boundary. Sometimes it means saying, "I don't know—but I'm willing to learn."

A Story: Three Places, One Lesson

Carlos was struggling on all fronts. At work, he felt unseen. At home, he felt misunderstood. In life, he felt like he was just going through the motions.

One day, a mentor told him: "No one is coming to fix this for you. But the good news is—you don't have to wait."

Carlos started asking different questions. He stopped waiting for permission. He began owning small actions: better communication at work, more presence at home, time each week for reflection and planning.

Nothing changed overnight. But eventually—everything did.

Key Takeaway

Ownership isn't just a mindset. It's a daily decision. At work, at home, and in life—real progress begins when you stop waiting and start leading yourself.

Reflection

Where in my life am I waiting for someone else to change before I take action?

_____

_____

_____

_____

_____

What's one area—work, home, or life—where I can take more ownership this week?

_____

_____

_____

_____

_____

What would it look like to lead myself, even if no one else does?

_____

_____

_____

_____

_____

CHAPTER 8

Moving from Victim to Leader

How to stop reacting and start choosing.

Bad things happen. Plans fall apart. People let us down. Opportunities slip by.

It's easy to feel powerless—like life is happening to us.

But there's a difference between being impacted by something and being defined by it. That's the difference between a victim mindset and a leader mindset.

One keeps you stuck. The other moves you forward.

What Is a Victim Mindset?

A victim mindset says:

- "There's nothing I can do."
- "People are out to get me."
- "Life is unfair."
- "Why does this always happen to me?"

It's not about whether bad things happened to you. They did. It's about how you interpret those experiences—and what you do next.

Victim thinking says, "This is why I can't." Leadership says, "Here's what I can do."

What Leadership Looks Like

You don't need a title to be a leader. You just need to own your choices.

A leadership mindset sounds like:

- "I don't like this, but I can choose how I respond."
- "This isn't my fault, but I'm responsible for my reaction."
- "I may not control everything, but I always control something."

Leadership isn't about being in charge of others. It's about being in charge of yourself.

A Story: The Team That Turned It Around

Angela led a customer support team. They were burned out. Complaints were high. Morale was low. She could have blamed upper management, staffing shortages, or the pandemic.

Instead, she got curious. She asked the team what was working—and what wasn't. She listened. She made small changes she could control: clearer shift handoffs, fewer unnecessary meetings, better recognition.

Slowly, things improved.

Angela didn't wait for permission to lead. She just started owning what was hers to improve—and invited others to do the same. That's leadership.

Shifting Out of Victim Mode

If you find yourself feeling helpless, try this process:

1. **Name the problem honestly.** What's really going on? Where do you feel stuck?

2. **Sort what you can and can't control.** List the facts. Circle what's in your power.
3. **Ask: "What's my next move?"** Leadership is often just taking the next right step.

Even if it's small. Even if it's hard. Even if no one's watching.

Common Victim Mindsets—and How to Flip Them

Victim Thought	Leadership Reframe
"No one supports me."	"Who have I asked for support—and how?"
"It's not my fault."	"What's still my responsibility?"
"They don't appreciate me."	"How can I advocate for myself?"
"I can't do anything about this."	"What one thing can I do?"

The shift isn't about blame—it's about agency.

A Story: The New Beginning

Mark had been laid off. Again. He was discouraged, angry, and tired of starting over. At first, he sat in the feeling. Blamed the company. Blamed the market.

But eventually, he asked: "What would a leader do—even in this situation?"

He updated his skills, reached out to his network, and started freelancing. It wasn't easy. But it moved him forward.

Victim mode waits for rescue. Leader mode starts walking.

Key Takeaway

You can't always choose what happens. But you can always choose how you respond. That's the beginning of leadership—and the end of helplessness.

Reflection

Where in my life am I acting like a victim—even subtly?

_____

_____

_____

_____

_____

What would it look like to lead myself in that area?

_____

_____

_____

_____

_____

What's one next right step I can take today?

_____

_____

_____

_____

_____

CONCLUSION

From Reaction to Ownership

We all face problems. But the people who make real progress—at work, at home, and in life—don't wait for someone else to fix things.

They take ownership. They stop blaming, stop explaining, and stop waiting. They lead themselves.

This book hasn't been about perfection. It's been about *practice.*

The practice of saying:

- "This part is mine."
- "This step is possible."
- "This change starts with me."

You've learned to:

- Spot the blame trap.
- Trade excuses for action.
- Focus on what you can control.
- Validate yourself instead of chasing approval.
- Rewrite your identity.
- Practice ownership in the real world.
- Shift from victim to leader.

These aren't one-time lessons. They're habits. They grow stronger each time you use them.

You won't always get it right. That's okay. Just keep coming back to the questions that matter:

- "What's mine to own?"
- "What can I do next?"
- "Who do I want to become?"

Because the moment you ask those questions, you stop being stuck.

And you start becoming someone who moves forward — on purpose.

Other Books in This Series

Your Problem Isn't Your Problem. Solve the right problem. Solve the root cause rather than treat symptoms.

What if the problem you're trying to solve isn't the real problem? Learn to distinguish between symptoms and causes. Challenge assumptions that limit your thinking. Take action that solves the root cause of problems.

My Problem Isn't Your Problem. Take responsibility for your problems. Don't blame, deflect, or expect others to fix your problems

Learn how to replace blame with responsibility, let go of excuses, and take real action at work, at home, and in your relationships. Shift from a victim mindset to one of leadership and agency.

Your Problem Isn't My Problem. Set healthy boundaries. Stop rescuing others and allow them to solve their own problems.

Understand when to help others and when to step back. Learn about setting boundaries, detaching emotionally from others' outcomes, and supporting others without enabling bad behavior.

About the Author

Larry Richman is a writer, speaker, and personal development coach known for his clear, practical approach to solving real-life challenges. With decades of experience helping individuals and organizations grow, he specializes in cutting through confusion to get to the heart of what really matters. His writing is refreshingly direct, relatable, and filled with tools you can use today to create lasting change.

www.ingramcontent.com/pod-product-compliance
Lightning Source LLC
Chambersburg PA
CBHW060625030426
42337CB00018B/3205